YOUR KNOWLEDGE HAS VALUE

Laura Herrmann

Attraction and Destination Management. A Summary

GRIN Verlag

Bibliografische Information der Deutschen Nationalbibliothek:

Die Deutsche Bibliothek verzeichnet diese Publikation in der Deutschen National-
bibliografie; detaillierte bibliografische Daten sind im Internet über http://dnb.d-
nb.de/ abrufbar.

Dieses Werk sowie alle darin enthaltenen einzelnen Beiträge und Abbildungen
sind urheberrechtlich geschützt. Jede Verwertung, die nicht ausdrücklich vom
Urheberrechtsschutz zugelassen ist, bedarf der vorherigen Zustimmung des Verla-
ges. Das gilt insbesondere für Vervielfältigungen, Bearbeitungen, Übersetzungen,
Mikroverfilmungen, Auswertungen durch Datenbanken und für die Einspeicherung
und Verarbeitung in elektronische Systeme. Alle Rechte, auch die des auszugsweisen
Nachdrucks, der fotomechanischen Wiedergabe (einschließlich Mikrokopie) sowie
der Auswertung durch Datenbanken oder ähnliche Einrichtungen, vorbehalten.

Imprint:

Copyright © 2013 GRIN Verlag GmbH
Druck und Bindung: Books on Demand GmbH, Norderstedt Germany
ISBN: 978-3-656-71235-0

GRIN - Your knowledge has value

Der GRIN Verlag publiziert seit 1998 wissenschaftliche Arbeiten von Studenten, Hochschullehrern und anderen Akademikern als eBook und gedrucktes Buch. Die Verlagswebsite www.grin.com ist die ideale Plattform zur Veröffentlichung von Hausarbeiten, Abschlussarbeiten, wissenschaftlichen Aufsätzen, Dissertationen und Fachbüchern.

Visit us on the internet:

http://www.grin.com/

http://www.facebook.com/grincom

http://www.twitter.com/grin_com

1. Please explain the following terms by also clarifying their independence: attraction, destination, activity.

- Play a vital part in encouraging visitors to a region (because of interaction with other tourism parts)
- Without attractions there would be a limited need for other tourism services;
- Some argue that tourism would not exist, if it were not for attractions.
- = "A designated permanent resource which is controlled and managed for the enjoyment, amusement, entertainment, and education of the visiting public.
- What is attraction?
  - Natural Environment;
  - Man made attractions (Tourist/ Non-tourist purpose)
  - Special Events
- Visitor attractions vs. Tourist attractions:
  - often called visitor attractions rather than tourist attractions
  - usually day visitors rather than staying visitors
  - visitors come from same region (surrounding area)
  - definition: tourist!
- Attractions vs. Destinations
  - Destinations are larger areas that include (a number of individual attractions / together with the support services required by tourists)
  - The existence of a major attraction tends to stimulate development of a destination
- Attractions, support services and facilities
  - Many attractions are increasingly developing services such as catering and accommodation on site to increase their income source
  - Some support services and facilities are attractions in their own right e.g. restaurants
  - Examples:
    - Orient Express (sell experience)
    - Concorde (sell experience)
    - Disneyland Resort Paris
    - Glacier Express
- Resort complexes (such as Disneyland Paris, Center Parks ...) blurring the distinction between attractions and destinations and attractions and support services
- Attractions vs. activities:
  - As far as activities are concerned, attractions are a resource that provide the raw material on which the activity depends.
  - Examples:
    - Boat cruise on Sydney Harbour
    - Scuba Diving on Great Barrier Reef
    - Skiing at Falls Creek
    - Rock climbing in Grampians National Park

2. Please explain Swarbrooke's model for destination development.

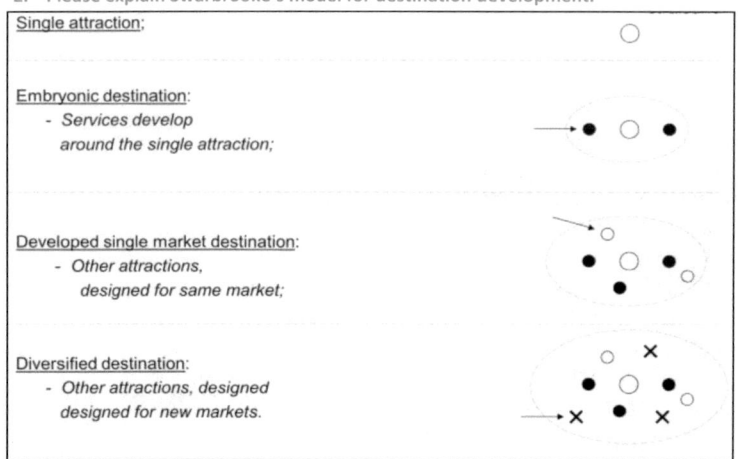

Single attraction;

Embryonic destination:
- Services develop
  around the single attraction;

Developed single market destination:
- Other attractions,
  designed for same market;

Diversified destination:
- Other attractions, designed
  designed for new markets.

As we saw in the previous chapter, popular attractions tend to grow into destinations and services such as hotels, restaurants and shops gather around the attraction to meet the needs of visitors. It could be said that attractions are the original grain of sand around which the destination 'pearl' grows. Most of the world's largest and most successful destinations developed from one major attraction. Thus Luxor's fame is based on its pyramids, Canterbury on its cathedral, Orlando on Disney World, and Oberammergau on its passion plays. The marketing of these destinations tends to focus on these attractions so that they are often the symbol of the destination in the minds of tourists. While some destinations remain based on a single attraction, such as Lourdes with its shrine, most develop new attractions to satisfy visitor demand and lengthen their stay. This latter pattern is perhaps best illustrated through Figure 2.1, although it must be observed that not all destinations pass through all these stages. This is obviously an idealized model that presupposes a Greenfield site with no existing development. In reality, most attractions are located within villages, towns or cities, with established services and infrastructure geared to the needs of residents. Clearly, the model relates to physical attractions rather than events and festivals. In due course, and in line with product life cycle theory, it may be that destinations may reach a fifth stage where some of the original attractions go into decline and the pattern of support services changes accordingly. Perhaps this phenomenon is already being seen in some British seaside resorts where entertainment facilities and other traditional attractions are closing and hotels are being converted into nursing homes. Until recently, there was in most destinations a clear distinction between attractions and support services including accommodation, catering and retailing. Most of the attractions and services were in the hands of separate owners in both the public and private sectors. Furthermore, it was generally quite easy in the past to distinguish between attractions and destinations. However, there are now a number of examples in Europe, and even more outside Europe, of attractions in the ownership of a single organization which are, in effect, destinations. They combine entertainment and support services on one site, albeit a very large site covering many hectares. A prime example of this is Disneyland Paris; such attractions are arguably destinations in their own right. Tourists feel no need to leave the site at all during their stay as it escapable of accommodating all their needs. There are now many such 'attractions' around the world, particularly in the USA and the countries of the Pacific Rim.

- Embryonic destination :
  - support services (e.g. hotels)
  - black dots: services

2

- Development single market destination:
  - same theme
  - black dots: newer attractions designed to appeal to the same market
- Diversified destination
  - diversify
  - black dots: new attractions designed to attract new markets to the destination
- Problem: get stuck with the existing image -> contradiction

3. Please give a brief overview on the concept of product life cycle.

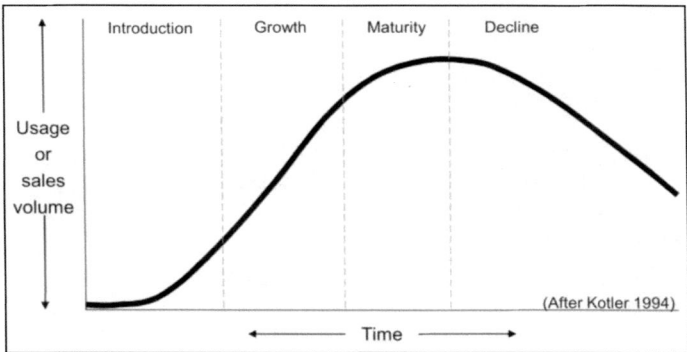

(After Kotler 1994)

- At each step product and its market have different characteristics that require different strategic marketing responses
- Problems:
  - The shape of the life cycle is not always the almost '5'-shaped curve; it may be bi-modal, namely with two peaks, or skewed, perhaps with growth not occurring until the last quarter of the timescale.
  - Product life cycles can vary dramatically in their time span. Staple products in traditional markets may have a life cycle measured in decades while products in fashion-conscious markets may last only a few weeks.
  - Many products never enter the growth stage. They are tested and fail and are therefore abandoned even though substantial investment may have been made in research and development.
  - Decline is not inevitable. Many products will be relaunched before they enter the decline stage. There is no guarantee that relaunches will be successful, although some products can have a number of relaunches so that their life-cycle curve looks like a succession of waves. Relatively few attractions fail at the introduction stage, although many attractions never get beyond the feasibility study stage

	Introduction stage	Growth stage	Maturity stage	Decline stage
Characteristics				
Sales	Low	Rapidly rising	Peak	Declining
Costs	High per customer	Average per customer	Low per customer	Low per customer
Profits	Negative	Rising	High	Declining
Customers	Innovative	Early adopters	Middle majority	Declining
Competitors	Few	Growing number	Stable number, beginning to decline	Declining
Marketing objectives		Create product awareness and trial	Maximize market share	Maximize profit while defending market shar	Reduce expenditure and 'milk' the brand
Strategies				
Product	Offer a basic product	Offer product extensions, service, warranty	Diversify brands and models	Phase out weak items
Price	Use cost-plus	Price to penetrate market	Price to match or better competitors	Cut price
Distribution	Build selective distribution	Build intensive distribution	Build more intensive distribution	Become selective: phase out unprofitable outlets
Advertising	Build product awareness amongst early adoptors and leaders	Build awarensee and interest in the mass market	Stress brand differences and benefits	Reduced to level needed to retain hard core of loyal customers
Sales promotion	Use heavy sales promotion to entice trial	Produce to take advantage of heavy consumer demand	Increase to encourage brand switching	Reduce to minimal level

4

4. Please explain the GAP-Model, while elaborating on the 5 specific gaps. Furthermore discuss how these (2-3) gaps can be managed in attraction management (how avoid that it appears / what to do when it happens).

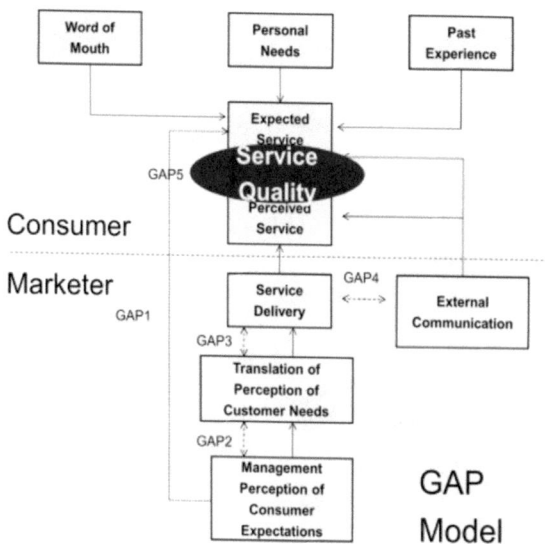

- Betont Umsetzungsproblematik

5. Chain of Critical Incidents
- Influencing factors for the visitor's experience

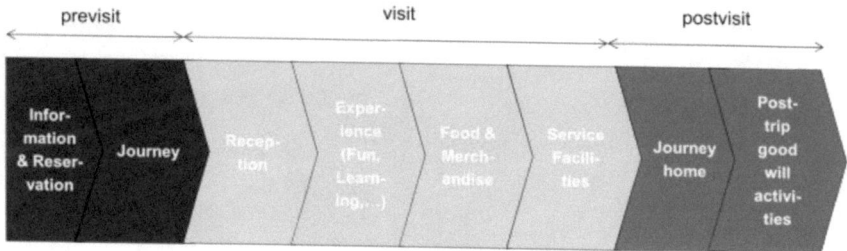

6. Name and describe the 3 dimensions of the Kano-Model, furthermore please explain and discuss the "quality challenge".

- Versucht Hierarchie zu schaffen
- Basic factors:
    - taken for granted
    - cannot lead to
    - satisfaction
    - unspoken
    - unconscious
- Performance:
    - explicit
    - bespoken
    - consciously
    - expected
- Delighters:
    - not expected
    - potential to differentiate from competition
- Quality challenge: Delighters -> Performance ->Basics (expectations constantly increasing), examples:
    - Babychange Facilities
    - Queuingtime at Tills
    - Online Offers / Webpage
    - In Flight movies
- No standardized product
    - difficult to adopt standardized quality control systems
    - affected by a number of variables
    - the product is different for every customer
- Intangibility and perishability
    - ,faults' in the product cannot be easily seen
    - not ease to replace a ,faulty' product
- Services are often complex products
    - involving a huge number of elements which are
    - interdependent and difficult to monitor
- Quality Development Wheel

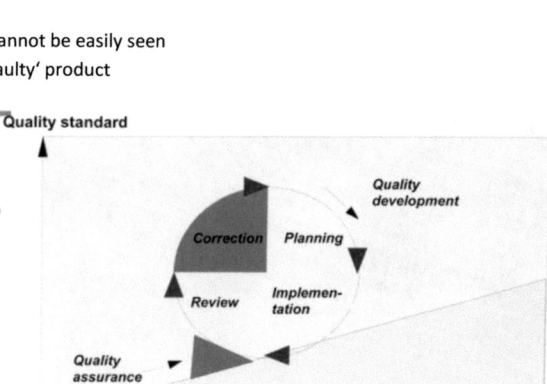

7. Discuss Pros and Cons of a Mystery Shopper Program.
- standardized questionnaire
- 4 times a year at key trading periods
- roughly at same time in all attractions
- run by independent external company
- PRO:
    - Independent
    - comes by surprise
    - sees business as it is
    - helps to monitor service standards
- CON:
    - only gives flash impression
    - human error occurs
    - individual perception is either not meassured at all, or not neutral

8. Discuss Pros and Cons of Capturing Customer Satisfaction data via electronic terminals.
- Method: post visit survey at computer terminal
- Touchscreen
- Set of up to 25 questions
- standardized accross all Merlin Attracions
- 9 KPIs (key peformance indicators): Satisfaction, Recommendation, Value for Money, Staff, Customer Service, Queuing, Food Service, Food Quality, Brand KPI
- other indicators: dwell time, catchment area, special product questions, repeatability, comment field, personal data
- PRO:
    - high data volume
    - low costs
    - data availability
    - quick to change / add / remove questions
    - comparability between attractions
- CON:
    - reliability
    - different factors affecting results (e.g. position of terminal)
    - access cannot be controlled (kids etc.)
    - evaluation on voluntary basis -> mostly extreme customers answer

9. Please define the term visitor management by also elaborating the four main problems supposed to be dealt with.

- visitor management incorporates aspects of both: quality management and green issues, and is the most critical part of the day-to-day management at the site
- Tries to ensure an experience without disturbances by providing a trouble-free sequence of events
- Aims to minimize negative environmental and socio-cultural impact caused by the use of the attr.

- Although most important for non-purpose built attractions, there is a certain relevance for all types of attractions

- Marketing – visitor expectations
- Profit, quality – management objectives
- Negative impacts in visitor management (Performance):
  - Disturbances (technical)
  - Overcrowding (limit of visitors, internal transport system, number of entrance points, infrastructure like toilets, food etc.)
- Problems to deal with
  - Damage on environment caused by visitors (wildlife, flora and fauna, pollution by traffic)
  - Damage on assets caused by visitors (intentional, unintentionally caused by heavy use)
  - Disturbances in visitor flow (bottleneck situations, waiting times)
  - Accessibility of certain areas (restricted access caused by construction work, distances between attractions on site, handicapped visitors)
- Identify problems
  - Legal conditions (waste management, pollution, opening time, ...)
  - Monitoring damages caused to assets (staff has to check, repair and report)
  - Damages to the environment (measure damages and report, often by externals)
  - Disturbances in visitor flow (tracking visitors)
  - Overall satisfaction of visitors (surveys and questionnaires)